OPEN SESAME English as a Second Language Series

BIG BIRD'S
YELLOW BOOK

Featuring Jim Henson's Sesame Street Muppets

Children's Television Workshop

Author

Jane S. Zion

Illustrators

Jonathan Burns

Mary Grace Eubank

David Gothard

Oxford University Press

1984

Oxford University Press

200 Madison Avenue
New York, NY 10016 USA

Walton Street
Oxford OX2 6DP England

OXFORD is a trademark of
Oxford University Press.

Library of Congress Cataloging in
Publication Data

Zion, Jane S.
  Big Bird's yellow book.

  (Open Sesame)
  Summary: Designed for children with
no prior knowledge of English to help
them develop listening and speaking
skills through conversations, songs,
chants, stories, and games based on
illustrations featuring various Muppet
characters.
  1. English language—Textbooks for
foreign speakers— Juvenile literature.
[1. English language—Textbooks for
foreign speakers] I. Burns, Jonathan,
ill. II. Eubank, Mary Grace, ill.
III. Gothard, David, ill. IV. Children's
Television Workshop. V. Title.
VI. Series.
PE1128.Z54 1984 428.3′4 83-25089
ISBN 0-19-434155-0

The publisher would like to thank Tom
Cooke for permission to reproduce
Meet the Muppets.

Printing (last digit): 9 8 7 6 5 4

Printed in Hong Kong

PREFACE

Big Bird's Yellow Book is for elementary school children beginning their study of English. Each of the lessons follows a carefully sequenced curriculum progressing from topic to function to structure. The functions and structures are correlated with topics that are particularly suitable for children, such as the family, the classroom, and the playground.

The focus is on oral-aural skills: there are no printed words. Children will develop their listening and speaking skills through songs, chants, conversations, poems, stories, and games all based on illustrations in the book. Visual cues at the top of each page indicate the purpose of each lesson.

Other components at this level include a Teacher's Book, an Activity Book, a Cassette, and Picture Cards.

 Song

 Chant

 Conversation between Muppets

 Share It Conversation between children

 Story

 Activity

 Test

CONTENTS

4

1.

2.

3.

4.

5.

6.

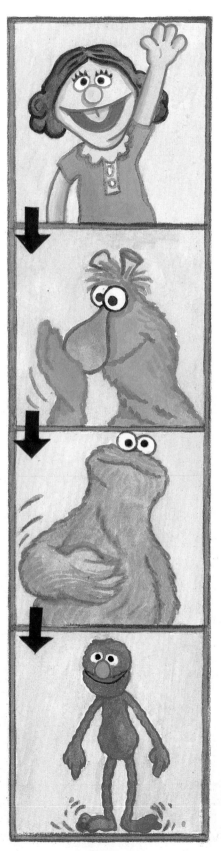

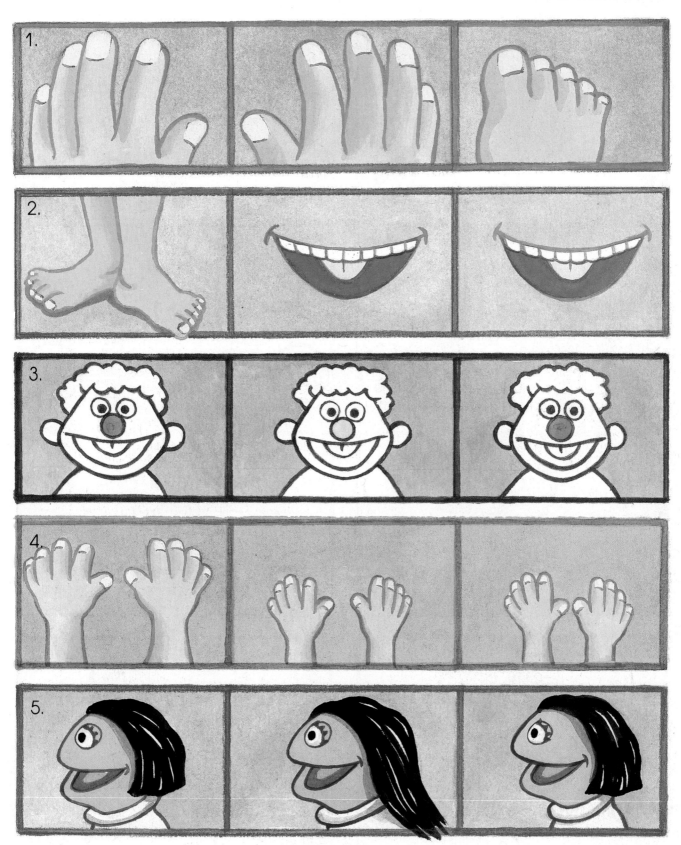

12

3

13

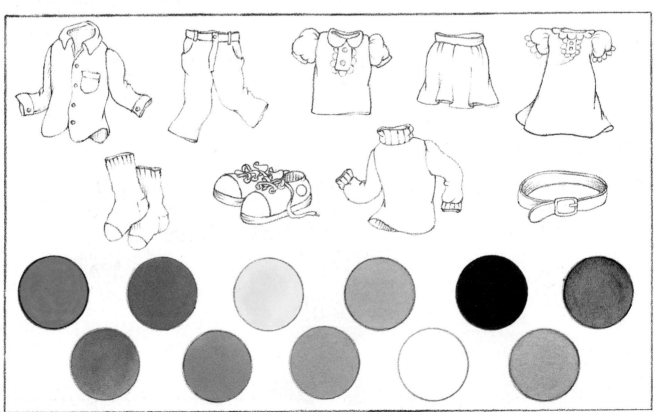

1.

2.

3.

4.

5.

6.

19

1.

2.

3.

4.

5.

6.

7.

8.

29

1.

2.

3.

4.

5.

6.

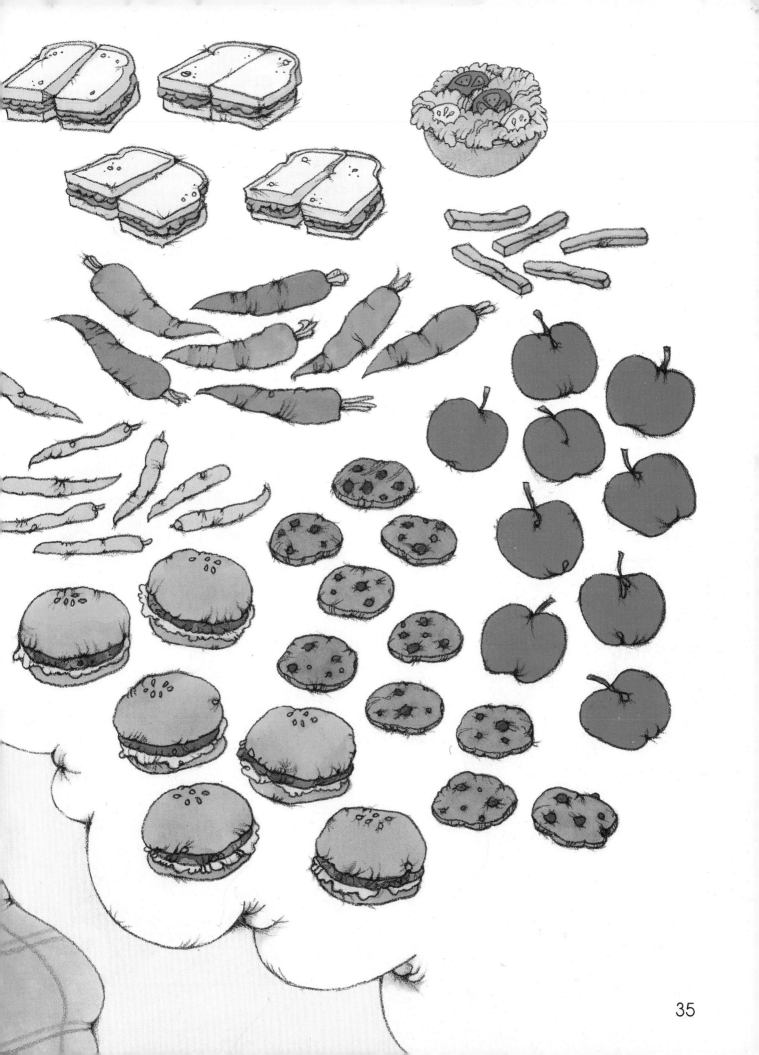

1.

2.

3.

4.

5.

6.

7.

8.

38

41

1.

2.

3.

4.

5.

6.

8

47

1.

2.

3.

4.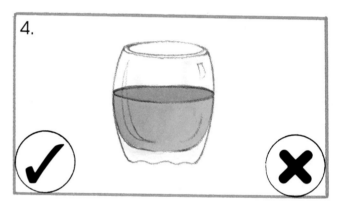

5.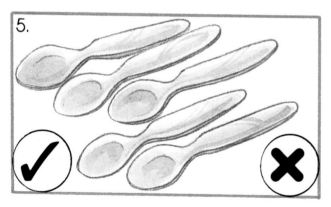

6.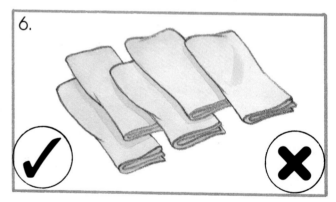

7.

8.

1.

2.

3.

4.

5.

6.

10

59

1.

2.

3.

4.

5.

6.